£5.99

## Imagine Drowning

'Mr Johnson is that rare creature – a moralist with wit.
He writes with responsible gaiety.'

*Guardian*

Set in a boarding house on the bleak Cumbrian coast, just up
the sands from Sellafield, **Imagine Drowning** is a compelling
drama of secrecy, violence and discovery, at once frightening
and funny. A journalist disappears while following up a story
about Sellafield. When his wife sets out to find him two weeks
later, she stays at the same boarding house, with its atmosphere
of unease, and meets the same menagerie of bizarre creatures.
As two intricate plots and time schemes intertwine, David and
Jane both discover the answers to some of their questions, while
the boarding house reveals a disturbing and intimate horror.

**Imagine Drowning** premièred at the Hampstead Theatre on
24 January 1991.

WITHDRAWN FROM
THE LIBRARY

UNIVERSITY OF
WINCHESTER

D0774460

## Other Methuen Modern Plays

include work by

Jean Anouilh
John Arden
Margaretta D'Arcy
Peter Barnes
Wolfgang Bauer
Brendan Behan
Edward Bond
Bertolt Brecht
Howard Brenton
Mikhail Bulgakov
Jim Cartwright
Caryl Churchill
Noël Coward
Sarah Daniels
Shelagh Delaney
David Edgar
Rainer Werner Fassbinder
Dario Fo
Michael Frayn
Max Frisch
Peter Handke
Vaclav Havel
Kaufman & Hart
Barrie Keeffe
Arthur Kopit
Larry Kramer
Franz Xaver Kroetz
Stephen Lowe
John McGrath
David Mamet
David Mercer
Arthur Miller
Mtwa, Ngema & Simon
Tom Murphy
Peter Nichols
Joe Orton
Louise Page
Luigi Pirandello
Stephen Poliakoff
David Rudkin
Willy Russell
Jean-Paul Sartre
Wole Soyinka
C. P. Taylor
Theatre Workshop
Peter Whelan
Nigel Williams
Victoria Wood

# Terry Johnson

# Imagine Drowning

Methuen Drama

## A Methuen New Theatrescript

First published in Great Britain in 1991
by Methuen Drama, Michelin House, 81 Fulham Road,
London SW3 6RB and distributed in the United States by
HEB Inc., 361 Hanover Street, Portsmouth, New Hampshire
03801 3959.

Copyright © 1991 by Terry Johnson

The author has asserted his moral rights

A CIP catalogue record for this book
is available from the British Library

ISBN 0-413-65250-5

*The front cover shows Le Double Secret by René Magritte © ADAGP,
Paris and DACS London, 1991. The photo of Terry Johnson on the back
cover is by Gill Fox.*

Printed in Great Britain
by Cox & Wyman Ltd, Cardiff Road, Reading

KING ALFRED'S COLLEGE
WINCHESTER

822.91
JOH          0123333bx

**Caution**

All rights whatsoever in this play are strictly reserved and
application for permission to perform it in whole or in part must be
made to Curtis Brown, 162–168 Regent Street, London W1R 5TB.

This book is sold subject to the condition that it shall not, by
way of trade or otherwise, be lent, resold, hired out, or otherwise
circulated without the publisher's prior consent in any form of
binding or cover other than that in which it is published, and
without a similar condition, including this condition, being
imposed on the subsequent purchaser.

**Imagine Drowning** was premièred at the Hampstead Theatre on 24 January 1991 with the following cast:

| | |
|---|---|
| **Jane** | Sylvestra le Touzel |
| **Brenda** | Frances Barber |
| **Tom** | Nabil Shaban |
| **David** | Douglas Hodge |
| **Buddy** | Ed Bishop |
| **Sam** | Daniel Evans |

*Directed by* Richard Wilson
*Designed by* Julian McGowan
*Lighting by* Rick Fisher

## Characters

**Jane**    Late twenties. County origins. A veneer of sophistication that only just hides her vulnerability.

**Brenda**    Late thirties. Cumbrian. A very slow woman, and quite uneducated. At times one might think her a little retarded, but that only reflects the degree to which she has chosen to participate in the world.

**Tom**    A substantially disabled man in his thirties. Very active. Very articulate.

**David**    Early thirties. Londoner. A tall, attractive man with a dark, brooding quality. He takes himself very seriously.

**Buddy**    A middle-aged middle-American. Softly spoken, quite self-absorbed.

**Sam**    Brenda's son. Under fifteen. All the attendant physical problems of the adolescent.

**Sophie**    Brenda's daughter. As young as possible.

## Setting

*A guest house near Gosforth in Cumbria. Beyond and around it; the shore, a barren coastline.*

*The front room has been knocked through to the back. The front door and staircase are visible, maybe the upstairs landing. Enough steps, doors, corners, nooks and crannies to give the impression of the classical haunted house transported to this specific time and location.*

*A few years ago, the house might have called itself a hotel. Now, it's hard to imagine any traveller staying more than one night.*

*The living room furnishings are faded, autumnal. A ruinous, saggy three-piece suite and other chairs all arranged with an easy view of the TV.*

*The TV is enormous.*

*The back of the VACANCIES/NO VACANCIES sign hanging in the window. An incongruous payphone.*

*A hatch to the kitchen, and under the stairs an old DIY attempt at a checking-in desk.*

*Toys litter the carpet.*

*There are only two strange signs of affluence; a video recorder and a complete set of* The Encyclopaedia Britannica.

*The room is also full to the brim with pets, or evidence of them. A cage for gerbils, a cage for mice. Two large aquaria with tubes and filters and paraphernalia. A budgie cage with too many budgies in it. A none-too-healthy parrot. Dog basket, cat litter.*

# Act One

## Prologue

*In the darkness, the Song of the Whale.*

*The aquaria light up, then the television (an undersea wildlife programme), then the rest of it. Greens and blues and motion that suggests deep water.*

*The characters are revealed in this submerged world. The swell of the water puts them in motion; small repeated gestures suggest images from the play we are about to see.*

*The lights change and* **Buddy** *appears on the beach with a lit paper moon, which he stakes into the sand.*

**Buddy** Grounded. Worse. Sent to England. To witness a sort of drowning. At first I was teaching young men to duck and weave through Cumbrian hills; less of an expert than an inspiration to those boys. And believe me, the morale of those young pilots from California and Kentucky had reached a pretty low ebb in and around Penrith, in England, in the late eighties, in the rain. So, having no further use for this particular brand of hero at home they shipped me over to remind those bored young bucks that even if they had decided on short acquaintance that the miserable English were really not worth defending, they were, like me, the US Airforce, and should be proud to fly over any godforsaken maniacally depressed country they were told to. And I counted those boys lucky, for they could do what I no longer could. They could fly. It had been decided that my flying days were long gone. I knew this, but the grey slate and the thumping rain to an earthbound soul made the earth unbearable. Briefly, I took to the bottle. Briefly. Then I took to the beach. They stood me down, I turned down their offer to fly me home again, and gave myself up to the magnetic pull of this magnificent shoreline. I tell you all this to explain my presence which in a practical sense is improbable. My own drama having played itself out twenty years ago, my role in this one was to be purely metaphysical. I knew nothing of its early scenes, except to be familiar with the dark and dreary boarding house that stood at the end of the esplanade. This was Brenda's house. She lived there with her children and her lodger Tom, who started the whole thing with some inadvisable call to the press. But this is not Tom's story, nor Brenda's (though you may have heard hers elsewhere). This is the story of Jane and David, who arrived on this bleak north-western coast two weeks apart, Jane looking for David, David looking for something even less tangible than himself. You could, I suppose, if you chose, ignore the rest of us. We are merely the Other People.

Scene One

*Lights up on the living room.* **Brenda** *alone, watching TV, 'This Is Your Life'.*

*The doorbell rings.* **Brenda** *uses the remote control to turn the TV down and answers the door. It's raining out.* **Jane** *is therefore sopping wet.*

**Jane** Hello.

**Brenda** Hello.

*A pause*

**Jane** I'm looking for a room.

**Brenda** (*very serious. Nods*) Mmm.

**Jane** I'm very wet.

**Brenda** You'd better come in.

**Jane** I might make a bit of a puddle, I'm sorry. Does it always rain this hard?

**Brenda** Yes, it's the weather.

**Brenda** *is neither welcoming nor hostile. She seems unused to guests.*

**Jane** Have you a room available?

**Brenda** Well, it is very quiet.

**Jane** Time of year I suppose?

**Brenda** No.

*Pause.*

**Brenda** We like it.

**Jane** What?

**Brenda** Quiet.

**Jane** Oh. I shan't be staying for long.

**Brenda** Holiday is it?

**Jane** No. Well, yes. See the sights.

**Brenda** Where?

**Jane** Well, do some walking. Nowhere in particular.

**Brenda** Well, the world's your lobster, isn't it?

**Jane** The world's my what?

**Brenda** Not lobster.

**Jane** Oyster.

**Brenda** That's it. Funny sort of fish for the world to be. You're meant to sign something. This is a sort of desk like a hotel if you do this. Feel silly. But you have to. There's a book somewhere. To sign. There's cotton sheets. Gas is all in no meter.

**Jane** Sea view?

**Brenda** No. Here we are then.

**Brenda** *opens the book.* **Jane** *signs.* **Brenda** *laughs a little laugh.*

**Brenda** Haven't had a Mz before. That means you're not married, does it?

**Jane***'s fingers move spontaneously to cover her wedding finger, on which is no ring.*

**Jane** No. No, it means it doesn't matter if I am or not.

**Brenda** Oh. I see.

**Brenda***'s hand covers her own ring finger, which* has *got a ring on it.*

**Brenda** It's a double bed.

**Jane** I'm on my own.

**Brenda** I'll go and put the sheets on. And the fire, take the chill out. You sit down here and get yourself warm. Make yourself at home. It's only a living room if there's no one. When there's someone it's the Television Lounge. You can watch the telly. Would you like to watch the telly?

**Jane** No thanks.

**Brenda** You can.

**Jane** Thanks. No.

**Brenda** Switch it off shall I?

**Jane** No, whatever.

**Brenda** 'This Is Your Life'.

**Jane** I see.

**Brenda** *stops still and watches. Television tends to mesmerize her.*

**Jane** Do you mind if I make a phone call?

**Brenda** Oh, I'm sorry. Please, do. I'll put a bottle in, just in case.

**Brenda** *goes upstairs and* **Jane** *goes to the phone.*

**Brenda** Give it a bang.

**Jane** *bangs the phone. The parrot is nearby.*

**Parrot** Hello.

*She decides not to answer. Dials.*

**Parrot** Do you love me? Do you? Do you love me?

**Jane** Mummy. It's me. / Yes, I know, I'm sorry. / I'm not coming. / No, I'm fine. I'm fine. I'm just not coming. / I am phoning. / I wasn't near a phone. I was on a train. / Cumbria. / I got a postcard from him. / Mummy, I know you'd be much happier if he was dead and gone but he's not. He's just . . . gone, somewhere, I don't know. I'll phone you soon. Well, put it in the deep freeze. / Well, mince it up for rissoles or something.

*A small but very grotesque monster pokes its head around a corner.*

**Jane** Mummy, don't start. Look, I'm in a box; there are people waiting. / No, I'm perfectly alright. Mummy, I am perfectly safe!

*She sees the monster and screams. It comes in and sits on the sofa. Reads a comic.*

**Jane** No, it's alright. I'm alright. I'm fine. No. Nothing. It was just a spider on the thingummy, that's all. You know what I'm like. / Yes I will. I promise. / Mummy, I promise. If I get murdered I'll call you, now bye bye.

*She puts the phone down.*

**Jane** You know, if I had a face like that, I'd wear a mask.

**Brenda** *returns.*

**Brenda** Sam! I told you. Bedroom.

*He goes.*

**Brenda** Thought you might like this.

**Jane** Thank you.

*Hands* **Jane** *a towel for her hair.* **Jane** *dries it,* **Brenda** *watches.*

**Brenda** And I've put the kettle on. Would you like a cup of tea?

**Jane** I'd love a cup of tea. Er, before you go . . . this postcard.

**Brenda** Yes?

**Jane** It's a photograph of this house, isn't it?

**Brenda** It's the esplanade. That's what they used to call it, when people came.

**Jane** My husband sent this to me. That's his writing.

**Brenda** Wish you were here. Ha ha. What does that mean then; ha ha?

**Jane** He has a funny sense of humour. He always sends me a postcard. I took this to the photographer's; their name is printed on the back. They directed me here. My husband's name is David Sinclair. David Sinclair. Do you know him?

**Brenda** No.

**Jane** This is his picture.

**Brenda** No.

**Jane** Are you sure?

**Brenda** Yes, I'm sure.

**Jane** He sent me this postcard. Are you absolutely positive?

**Brenda** No. I mean, yes. I mean I've never seen him in my life, no.

**Jane** It would only have been a couple of weeks ago. He's a journalist.

**Brenda** I'm sorry.

**Jane** Damn. If I hadn't come so far I'd turn right round and go back.

**Brenda** Yes. I would if I had.

**Jane** I'll die of pneumonia if I don't get out of these things.

**Brenda** Your room's at the top of the stairs. First on the left. I'll bring you up the tea?

**Jane** No, it's alright. I'll come down.

**Jane** *picks up her suitcase and goes upstairs. Kettle boils offstage.* **Brenda** *leaves. The doorbell rings.* **Brenda** *returns, without her cardigan on. Opens the door. Bright evening sunshine.* **David** *is at the door.*

(AS WELL AS BEING WITH **Jane**, WE SHALL SPEND TIME WITH **David** ON HIS VISIT A FEW WEEKS EARLIER. THE QUALITY OF LIGHT IS ALL THAT INDICATES THIS DOUBLE TIME SCHEME.)

**David** Hello. Does um, Tom Dudgeon live here?

**Brenda** Um.

**David** My name's David Sinclair. I was given this address.

**Brenda** Oh, Yes. He's not in.

**David** Oh. It says on the window vacancies. Does that mean there's a room I could . . .

**Brenda** What?

**David** Stay in?

**Brenda** Oh. Of course. Yes. You'll have to sign the book.

**David** Fine. Will he be back soon?

**Brenda** Never know with Tom.

**David** Is there a phone?

**Brenda** A pippy phone.

**David** In the room?

**Brenda** Over there.

**David** Right.

*He goes to the phone.*

**Brenda** Give it a bang.

*He does, then dials.*

**Brenda** Will you be wanting breakfast?

**David** Oh, coffee, croissant.

**Brenda** Yes. How many eggs?

**David** Alright, two.

**Brenda** Bacon, sausage and tomatoes. Full English breakfast.

**David** Delicious. Hello, Bob? It's David. / I'm in Cumbria.

**Brenda** *leaves*.

**David** Cornwall? No, I came north. Edge of nowhere. / What the hell ever happens in Cornwall? / Oh, send Stuart; I can't make Cornwall, I'm in bloody Cumbria. / I did tell the office. I told Tish. / Bob, you didn't have a story for me and when this guy called you were still out to lunch. / I don't know yet. Some sort of protest at Sellafield. / Tomorrow morning, first thing. I did what I thought you'd want me to do! / Look, this is ridiculous. Are you seriously suggesting I take the milk train to cover Her Majesty the Prime Minister opening another fucking ring road? I could do that from here, for Christ's sake. / Bob, do you know how far away Plymouth is? / I know trains run all night, they're where I usually sleep. / Alright. I'll get the bloody train. But when a gang of maniacs cut the wire and go apeshit in Sellafield and my arse is in Cornwall, you can kiss it.

*Puts the phone down. Dials again.*

**Parrot** Hello.

**David** *ignores it. Phone is answered.*

**David** Hello?

**Parrot** Hello.

**David** Fuck off. Hello? Can you put me through to Andrew Norris please. (*To* **Parrot**.) Fuck off. Come on, after me. Fuck off. Fuck off.

**Parrot** Fuck off!

**David** Well done. Andrew? David. / Sinclair. Listen Andy, I'm calling in that favour. I want you to file a story for me. / Thatcher opening the ring road. / Andy, you don't have to be there. Just type up the first agency report, snide reference to the quality of life on the M25, and put my name on it. / I might not be near a phone. I'm having a sniff around something. As a matter of fact, yes. / Wouldn't you like to know. Just cover my bum, will you? / Thank you, Andrew. Quits. Bye.

**David** *sees a pile of postcards on the desk-flap.*

**Brenda** *enters with a towel.*

**Brenda** Here's a towel, it's included.

**David** Are these of here?

**Brenda** Yes.

**David** Seen better days.

**Brenda** I know.

*He takes a postcard.*

**Brenda** For the animals.

**David** What?

*She lifts and junkles her RSPCA collection box.*

**David** Oh.

*He donates. She gives him the key.*

**David** See you later then.

**Brenda** Yes. Will you be staying long?

**David** Only tonight.

*He picks up his suitcase and word processor and goes upstairs.*

*Kettle boils offstage.* **Brenda** *disappears briefly and returns with her cardigan on and a tray of tea.*

**Jane** *descends.*

**Jane** It's a lovely room.

**Brenda** (*Surprised*) Is it alright?

**Jane** And there is a sea view.

**Brenda** No.

**Jane** If you stand on tiptoe and look out of the top window, between the roofs, a little blue triangle.

**Brenda** Well I never.

**Jane** Well, grey, a very small triangle.

**Brenda** I was going to say. I'd have noticed that. Here we are then. Lovely cup of tea.

**Parrot** Lovely cup of tea.

**Brenda** Cheeky devil.

**Jane** (*Smiles*) What's his name?

**Brenda** Moby Dick.

**Jane** Isn't that a fish?

**Brenda** No, a cockatoo.

**Jane** You like animals?

**Brenda** I love animals.

**Jane** *finds a perspex thingummy on the mantelpiece.*

**Jane** What's this?

**Brenda** Ant farm.

**Jane** Eurgh. Where are the ants?

**Brenda** Don't know. Sam left the top off.

**Jane** Highly sophisticated social order, ants.

*She sits on the sofa.*

**Brenda** All buggered off in a long line across the carpet. There's a hamster too, somewhere. In the sofa probably.

**Jane** *gets up from the sofa.*

**Jane** What's in here?

**Brenda** Gerbils. Don't lift the lid.

**Jane** I wasn't going to.

**Brenda** Gerbils jump.

**Jane** You don't let them out then?

**Brenda** Well, Sophie's not allowed to play with the gerbils. She loves them too hard. Sends them bye byes. And they stay a bye byes until I can get down the petshop.

**Jane** You should try to explain it to her, surely.

**Brenda** What?

**Jane** Death.

**Brenda** I didn't know there was an explanation.

**Jane** *starts to cry.*

**Jane** Sorry. This is stupid. I'm just very tired. He never phoned. His paper doesn't care; he let them down on something or other. His editor suggested I look in the nearest gutter. I've been to the police. He doesn't qualify as a missing person, until he turns up dead or something, I don't know. All I've got is this stupid bloody postcard. Sorry.

**Brenda** He never came home? Your husband?

**Jane** No.

**Brenda** *crosses herself.*

**Jane** Was he here?

**Brenda** I have tried with Sophie. I tried to tell her why we had to bury the rabbit. She understood until Friday then dug it up again to see if it was hungry. No, nothing dies in this house. They just change colour. 'Mummy, why is Moby Dick white when he was green yesterday?' Because he had his feathers changed, my love. He had a change of heart.

*She goes to the parrot.* Tell me you love me.

**Parrot** *gives a low rumbling squawk.*

**Brenda** Do you?

**Parrot** Love you.

**Brenda** *smiles at* **Jane**.

**Jane** Thanks for the tea.

**Jane** *goes upstairs.*

*The weather changes.*

*A key in the lock and* **Tom** *enters in his wheelchair with a bag full of loofahs.*

**Brenda** Tom?

**Tom** Only me.

**Brenda** Tom, there's a man.

**Tom** Is there?

**Brenda** Yes. There is. There's a man to see you. Who is he, Tom?

**Tom** Until I meet him, Brenda, it's hard for me to say. Here.

*He hands her a small package.*

**Brenda** What is it?

**Tom** For the children.

**Brenda** What is it?

**Tom** Guess.

**Brenda** Water wings.

**Tom** That's astonishing.

**Brenda** I'm right?

**Tom** No, you're completely wrong. But so was I. I thought it was water wings too. Blow it up.

**Brenda** *inflates the gift. It is a globe of the earth in coloured vinyl plastic.*

**Tom** I bought it without looking. I had no idea. Don't let her use it in the water. If she lost her grip she could drown.

**Brenda** It's beautiful, Tom. It's not water wings, no. But it's beautiful.

**David** *comes downstairs.*

**David** Sorry. Hello. Is there a pub?

**Brenda** This is the man, Tom.

**David** Tom? Tom Dudgeon?

**Tom** Hello.

**David** Hello. Sorry. David Sinclair.

**Tom** Pleased to meet you. This is Brenda.

**David** We've met.

**Brenda** Hello.

**David** Hello.

*Pause.*

**David** Are there any sheets?

**Brenda** Sheets?

**David** For the bed.

**Brenda** Oh, I'm sorry. I'm so, so sorry.

**David** That's alright.

**Brenda** I'm so terribly sorry.

**Tom** Brenda.

**Brenda** What?

**Tom** Don't castigate yourself.

**Brenda** No. What?

**Tom** Just put some sheets on the bed.

**Brenda** Right. (*Whispers to* **David**.) I'm sorry, really. I am so sorry.

**David** It's alright, really.

*She leaves.* **Tom** *takes loofahs out of the bag and piles them on a table.*

**Tom** Thanks for coming.

**David** It had better be worth it.

**Tom** The only newspaper in this town is strictly weddings and netball.

**David** You said there was going to be a demonstration. How big?

**Tom** Pretty big for these parts.

**David** Outside the plant?

**Tom** Where else?

**David** Inside?

**Tom** Perhaps. I'll give you a lift out there in the morning.

**Brenda** *comes back with sheets.*

**David** Thank you. What in?

**Tom** I drive a mini.

**Brenda** Tom's a very good driver.

**David** Well, you'd have to be, I suppose. Is there a pub?

**Tom** Just down the road.

**David** Could we talk there?

**Tom** Certainly.

**David** I'll get my notebook.

**David** *leaves*.

**Brenda** Who is he, Tom?

**Tom** It's alright, Brenda.

**Brenda** Works for the papers.

**Tom** For the good papers. I need him. Don't worry yourself.

**Brenda** Trust you.

**Tom** Yes. You can.

**David** *comes downstairs*. **Brenda** *goes into the kitchen*.

**David** Why me, anyway?

**Tom** How many good left-wing journalists are there?

**David** You know the paper I work for has just changed hands? Assurances of editorial freedom of course, but I can't guarantee they'll print anything unless you hack a copper to death.

**Tom** That bad?

**David** Getting worse.

**Tom** Will you resign?

**David** No. Time was.

**Tom** What changed?

**David** I did.

*They leave.*

**Jane** *comes downstairs quietly. Looks in the register.*

**Brenda** *enters from the kitchen wheeling* **Tom**. *He carries a tea tray.*

**Jane** *closes the book hurriedly.*

**Brenda** Oh.

**Jane** Hello. I was um . . .

**Brenda** This is Tom. This is the woman, Tom.

**Tom** Hello.

**Jane** Hello.

**Tom** My impersonation of a tea trolley.

**Jane** Very good.

**Tom** Thank you.

**Brenda** *pours.*

**Tom** Welcome to Cumbria.

**Jane** Thank you.

**Tom** Brenda tells me you're looking for a man.

**Jane** I'm looking for my husband. David Sinclair.

**Tom** Is he blind?

**Jane** Blind? No.

**Tom** Only David Sinclair I knew was blind. Met him in disabled school. It was a lot of fun having him push my chair about. None of the staff thought it was much fun, but the spazzers cheered up no end. 'Left hand down a bit, David!' Crash. He was deaf in one ear, you see.

**Jane** Yes. I see.

**Tom** He once asked me to describe the moon to him. That was depressing. Not because I failed but because his curiosity was infectious. What must it be like? Riding about on those leggy things you've all got. Lurching along, masters of your ship, not lashed to the wheel. Whatever the weather, at one with those two tree-trunk galleons.

**Jane** Yes. I um . . .

**Brenda** You don't want to listen to Tom. There's something wrong with his cephalic index, that's what it is.

**Jane** Oh, I'm sorry.

**Tom** Taught me a lot did David's curiosity.

**Jane** Discontent?

**Tom** Imagination.

**Brenda** Oh, imagination. I sometimes wish I had that. Just imagine.

**Jane** Two weeks ago my David went off on the assignment and that's the last I saw of him.

**Tom** Have you tried the police?

**Jane** They told me to wait ten days.

**Tom** Ten days?

**Jane** Length of a cheap package holiday. But he's not abroad. He came north, I'm sure of that.

**Tom** Well, he didn't stay here.

**Jane** You are sure?

**Tom** Why should we lie? Have you been married long?

**Jane** Four years. Why?

**Tom** Happy ever after?

**Jane** He stayed somewhere in this town. Tomorrow I'll try the other hotels.

**Tom** Shouldn't take you long.

**Jane** (*rises, stops*) Is there a pub?

**Tom** Other side of town.

**Jane** I'll find him if it kills me.

*Grabs her coat and leaves.*

**Brenda** Tom . . .

**Tom** Shhh. Cephalic index?

**Brenda** It's a real word.

**Tom** I'm impressed.

**Brenda** I'd rather have an Imagination. If I did I'd do all sorts of things in my head. Skiing. Snow. Drive a car.

**Tom** Climb a ladder.

**Brenda** In a forest with monkeys.

*Stops, embarrassed.*

**Tom** Go on.

**Brenda** Go in a cave. Find a four leaf clover. Looked though. Play the piano. Whatsit, banjo. Ghost train.

**Tom** Easy. Just climb on.

**Brenda** No. I never could. I've picked flowers. But smoked salmon.

**Tom** What?

**Brenda** In Safeways.

**Tom** Smoked salmon?

**Brenda** I almost though. Lots of times.

**Tom** Go on.

**Brenda** I couldn't. Never even done cat's cradle. When I was small. Brought it home, cat's cradle. Couldn't do it. Got my fingers tangled. Got all tangled up.

**Brenda** *panics.*

**Brenda** Tom. . .!

**Tom** It's alright.

**Brenda** But she . . . what if she . . .

**Tom** It's OK. It's alright. He's gone.

**Brenda** He might have . . .

**Tom** He might have got a little bit wet, that's all.

*Pause.*

**Brenda** Oh Tom. Listen to that rain.

*Lights fade.*


Scene Two

*Evening.* **Tom** *and* **David** *arrive from the pub.* **David** *is drunk.*

**David** When the really bad news began . . . South Africa, 1985, I was there. My first serious foreign assignment. If they'd known how serious it was going to get they'd have sent someone older. Someone like Stephenson. He was there; this Fleet Street legend, pissed old cynic, I hated him. When the worst started there were twelve of us in a hotel television lounge sending out the most fantastic stuff. A dozen of us yelling down the only three phone lines. Runners coming in with eye-witnesses. A fourteen-year-old boy dripping blood on my word-processor, I remember, wouldn't go wash up, wanted to tell us, wanted us to tell. The din, the adrenalin. You've never felt anything like it. Then four days later the lines were down, metaphorically I mean. Everything was D notice. It piled up until we stopped collecting. Material that would have made a dozen colour supplements, let alone the actual news, and no way to pass it out without the actual risk of actual arrest, and – we had the evidence – of actual torture. I was desperate to get this stuff out, but after a couple of days the hotel lounge had come to a full stop. All these so called foreign correspondents sitting around drinking iced coffee. Only topic of conversation seemed to be where to get your laundry done. Stephenson sat there. He could see I was furious.

He put down his glass, and said, 'You hear that noise?'
'What noise?'
It was silent as the grave.
I said, 'What noise?'
He looked at the dead typewriters and the comatose phones and he said, 'The silence. Do you know what that silence is?'
I said no.
He said, 'Genocide. The silence is genocide.'

**Tom** You used that line. I remember reading that.

**David** It's a very good line. Tight, perceptive, emotive. It had the desired effect on me. I exploded. A torrent of righteous indignation. How dare we all just fucking sit there! We are the voice of these people. It's our job to break the silence! Stephenson smiled, and passed me the phone. We had been forbidden to ask for an outside line. We both knew I might be arrested. Silenced. And I did not have the courage to pick up that phone. And I knew that my life up until that moment had been rhetoric. That whatever I believed or said or said I believed . . . it was just words. I was what mattered. The only really important thing in my life was me.

I once interviewed Enoch Powell. He was defending strong government. He said he believed that man was primarily self-centred, thus incurably greedy and inevitably violent to his fellow man. I said wasn't that a pretty pessimistic view of humanity?

He said, 'Of course. I'm a pessimist. That's why I'm a Tory.'

*A physical display of anger from* **David**. *Pent up, unexpressable.*

**Tom** Why does that upset you so much?

**David** I'm a pessimist too. I find it hard to imagine a world without winners and losers. It's like pissing in the wind trying to help the blacks, the unemployed, the crippled, sorry, the disenchanted, disenfranchised, the bloody Rainbow Alliance for Christ's sake; the losing side . . . Oh, battles have been won, revolutions have been staged to reorganise the corruption . . . but for 10,000 years the losers have fought and lost and lived and lost and lost and lost again . . . Socialism didn't die last week; it never drew its first breath.

**Tom** Stalin saw to that. True socialism . . .

**David** Is a dream!

**Tom** Well, capitalism's a fucking nightmare.

**David** It was never real! Reality isn't what we hope for or work for or imagine. Reality is the concrete world we live in. Reality is solid. This is reality.

*He bangs his fist on the coffee table. It collapses.*

**David** Shit.

**Tom** Nothing's certain. There are no immovable objects, no irresistible forces.

**David** *takes some volumes of* The Encyclopaedia Britannica *and props up the table.*

**Tom** What are you doing?

**David** I'm mending the table.

**Tom** It'll never be good as new. Second Law of Thermodynamics. The table's doomed to wobble from now on. Eventually it'll all fall down.

**David** Bollocks. There you go. Solid as a rock.

**Tom** Revolution is the only viable alternative. A new table.

**Tom** *throws* **David** *the globe.* **David** *heads for the stairs with it.*

**David** Then what? Who sits around the table? Who gets to eat at the fucking table?

**Tom** Why are you angry at me? Be angry at them.

**David** There's a bit of them in all of us, God knows! I can feel it. Can't you feel it? A black and bloody nugget in us all.

*He has gone.*

**Tom** *goes to the dining table and begins painting a placard in red paint, which will eventually read 'SOUTH AFRICAN BLOOD BATH'.* **Jane** *arrives through the front door with a bottle of Scotch.*

**Tom** Hello.

**Jane** You startled me.

**Tom** Only said hello.

**Jane** I don't usually drink. Didn't want to die of pneumonia.

**Tom** Worse things to die of. Found him yet?

**Jane** No.

**Tom** Town this size, if you haven't yet you're not likely to.

**Jane** You sound as if you don't much care.

**Tom** Why should I?

**Jane** You're very rude. Have a drink.

**Tom** Go to bed.

**Jane** Just a small one.

**Tom** I am the envy of many alcoholics, being legless even before my first drink, which means my alcohol level is well above the brain before you can say Jack Daniels. So if I drank with you I'd end up on the carpet, and you'd have to pick me up and take me beddybyes.

*He waggles his tongue lasciviously.*

**Jane** You don't like me, do you?

**Tom** Go to bed.

**Jane** It's very hard to talk with you.

**Tom** You should try dancing.

**Jane** I keep feeling I ought to be polite all the time, but you don't deserve it. You're not polite. In fact, you're not even very nice.

**Tom** Don't be silly. Disabled people are extremely nice. I haven't always been like this. I was a Buddhist monk in a previous incarnation.

**Jane** What happened?

**Tom** I must have raped a nun or something. Fucked it right up, anyway. I wish I'd re-incarnated in the East. I would have been treated like a minor deity, not shit on wheels.

**Jane** I've treated you like a perfectly normal person.

**Tom** Well you'd have to. This one's *articulate* shit on wheels. Step on me, I not only mess up your shoe, I also criticise your taste in footwear.

**Jane** I do think you're very brave.

**Tom** Oh Christ. Look, I moved north to get away from platitudes like that. Up here there are no disabled toilets but there are plenty of blokes who'll throw me over their shoulder and carry me in.

**Jane** I spend my life apologising for not being working-class.

**Tom** God, give me strength.

**Jane** But if you insist on being so damn superior . . .

**Tom** I just can't stand it when people . . .

**Jane** Then people are going to be superior back at you.

**Tom** . . . 'make an effort'.

**Jane** Yes I was. But for my sake, not yours. I need a friend.

**Tom** And presumably so does the physically handicapped person.

**Jane** I give up.

**Parrot** Hello.

**Jane** Hello.

**Parrot** Do you love me?

**Jane** I hardly know you. Do you love me? Say I love you. Come on. I love you. Tell me, I love you.

**Parrot** Fuck off.

**Jane** *is inordinately upset*.

**Tom** Are you alright?

**Jane** What upsets me is how you sit there . . . liking yourself so much. I mean, I'm a very nice person. I am. And I fucking hate me. God, I'm pissed.

**Parrot** *squawks*.

**Jane** Oh, fuck off yourself.

**Tom** Did you tell David to fuck off?

**Jane** No I fucking didn't because I don't fucking swear. Who taught a nice innocent creature disgusting words like that?

**Tom** I don't know.

**Jane** David swore. When I met him he was the most articulate man I ever met. Just before he left all I ever heard was f this, bugger that, sod you.

**Tom** It's late. I'm off to bed. Busy day tomorrow.

*He goes towards his room.*

**Jane** There's a pub just around the corner. You said the nearest pub was across the town. Why did you say that?

**Tom** Had to get you out of the house.

**Jane** Why?

**Tom** Hide the body.

**Jane** Ha. Ha.

*He has gone. She drinks, shivers. Goes back to the register, but is interrupted again by a thump from the top of the stairs.*

**Jane** Who's there?

*She goes to the stairs to investigate. No one. Turns to walk away. A man's head comes bumping down the stair. She stifles a scream.* **Sam** *laughs from upstairs. She investigates the head. It's rubber, faintly recognisable as* **David**.

**Sam** *runs downstairs, picks up the head, and runs back to bed.*

**Sam** Were you scared?

**Jane** Yes thank you.

*He goes. She drinks. Lights fade.*


Scene Three

*Lights come up for the next morning.* **Tom** *is very busy.* **Jane** *runs down the stairs for breakfast.*

**Jane** Good morning.

**Tom** Good morning. You're too late.

**Jane** For what?

**Tom** Breakfast.

**Jane** That's alright, I couldn't.

**Tom** I need your help.

**Jane** What sort of help?

**Tom** We're going shopping. We'll need this, this and this.

*He hands her a can of red paint, a screwdriver and a large handwritten notice that says 'SOUTH AFRICAN BLOODBATH'.*

**Jane** Why? What?

**Tom** I need you to wheel me to the doorway of Sainsbury's, dump me, then wheel the chair away and out of sight. If the law show up before you've made your move, abort the mission. If they show up later keep your head down and get as many photos as you can.

*He hands her a camera.*

**Jane** I take dreadful photos. I cut people's heads off.

**Tom** Then you'll probably get me centre frame.

**Jane** Well no, really, actually I feel a bit sick.

**Brenda** *comes in with* **Jane**'s *breakfast.*

**Brenda** Full English breakfast.

**Jane** Oh God. Thank you.

**Brenda** Are you going out, Tom?

**Tom** Yes.

**Brenda** Are you coming back or will you be at the police station again?

**Tom** Not sure.

**Brenda** I'll do a salad.

**Brenda** *exits.*

**Jane** Are you going to do something illegal?

**Tom** (*yells*) The fruit in this store was grown on stolen land!

**Jane** God, my head.

**Tom** The tinned fruit was canned by black slave labour!

**Jane** Tom, please.

**Tom** The money you pay for it directly funds the oppression of the black South African majority!

**Jane** Please. Save the world if you must, but do it quietly. I can't eat this.

*She goes to the kitchen.* **David** *comes downstairs.*

**Tom** Get your anti-nuclear loofahs here! Get yourself well scrubbed. Reaches the parts other decontaminating agents cannot reach. Get your anti-nuclear loofah here!

**David** Shut up for Christ's sake.

**Tom** Good morning.

**David** You know why the Russian revolution failed? Vodka. That's why the Russian revolution failed.

*Enter* **Brenda** *with more breakfast.*

**Brenda** Full English breakfast.

**Brenda** *exits.* **David** *looks at breakfast.*

**David** Don't suppose it's time to go, is it?

**Tom** If you like.

**David** I need some fresh air.

**Tom** I'll follow you. Take this.

*Gives* **David** *the bag of loofahs*.

*Exit* **David,** *enter* **Jane**.

**Tom** Ready?

**Jane** What for?

**Tom** To actually *do* something, you great lump of entropy.

**Jane** Why me? Why not Brenda?

**Tom** Brenda doesn't like the police.

**Jane** Oh well then, that's alright. I love the police. I especially love them arresting me.

**Tom** Coming?

**Jane** Why should I?

**Tom** Do you think the systematic oppression of black people is a good thing.

**Jane** No. Of course not.

**Tom** And are you doing anything else of global importance this morning?

**Jane** No.

**Tom** Well then.

**Jane** If my father was alive he'd spin in his grave.

*They leave.*

**Brenda** *comes on with a bowl of cat food and a bowl of dog food. Puts them on the floor. Picks up a paper bag and takes out a new tub of fish food.*

**Brenda** (*reads*) Float some on top of the water, as much as your fishes like.

*Turns on TV.*

**Brenda** The fishes will eagerly devour it.

*Opening credits of Australian soap on TV.* **Brenda** *feeds the fish. The lights fade.*


Scene Four

*Lights up in the living room.*

*The TV is on.*

**Sam** *is sitting at the table. He has a death-mask on his face, in fact a plaster of Paris mould. Two straws stick out from under his nose.*

**David** *dashes in. His trousers are muddy from the knee down. He has been walking miles. He is exhausted, frustrated, and angry. Rushes to the phone. Hasn't got any change. Goes over to* **Sam.**

**David** Have you got any . . . Jesus Christ. What the hell are you doing?

*It looks at him.*

**David** Never mind.

*He runs upstairs.*

**Jane** *arrives through the front door.*

**Jane** Hello. Jesus Christ. What the hell are you doing?

*It looks at her.*

**Jane** You're Sam, aren't you? I'm Jane. Brenda! Is your mother in? Would she mind if I made a cup of tea? What are you doing?

**Sam** (*indistinct*) How can I answer you when I can't move my mouth?

**Jane** Sorry.

*She goes into the kitchen.*

**Sam** *taps the mask to see that it's set, then peels it off.* **David** *comes downstairs and screams outrageously at the face underneath.*

**Sam** Very funny.

**David** What are you doing?

**Sam** I'm making a video nasty.

**David** A what?

**Sam** Don't tell my mother. She'd go apeshit.

**David** I'm not surprised

*Goes to the phone and dials.*

**David** What's making a video nasty got to do with dipping your head in a bowl full of gunk?

**Sam** I'm making a head cast, what do you think? It's special effects, this.

**Jane** *returns.*

**Jane** That's an improvement. So, what are you doing?

**Sam** I'm making a head cast.

**Jane** Sounds disgusting.

**Sam** Well as a matter of fact, horror film technology has revolutionised medical prosthetics.

**Jane** Prosthetics?

**Sam** Rubber bits.

**Jane** This is a hobby, is it?

**Sam** Yes. The last one I made was hopeless. The first one I made someone sat on.

*He points to the head that* **Jane** *encountered previously.*

**Sam** Hardly lifelike at all. I'm getting better.

**Jane** And what's the end result?

**Sam** A video nasty. Sex and violence.

**Jane** Sex as well?

**Sam** Yeh. I do know about sex.

**Jane** I'm sure you do.

**Sam** But I can't find a girl that knows how to scream properly. Plenty of blokes at school know how to push them down and get on top of them but I can't find a good screamer. They all keep on giggling. I can't stand girls. Don't tell my mother. She hates the things I like.

**Jane** I can't imagine why.

*Kettle whistles,* **Jane** *exits.*

**David** Hello, Tish? David Sinclair. Am I on a job this afternoon? / Talk to Bob, why? / Well, I'm in, um Cornwall, why? / Bob! Hi Bob. / I'm in um, Cornwall. / Look I filed a hundred words, have . . . / You got them? Good. / What? / What? / Jesus. Bob, I'm having trouble hearing you. This is a very bad line. Can I call you back? / I'll call you back.

*Puts phone down.*

**David** Jesus H. Christ.

*Dials again.*

**Jane** *returns with tea.*

**Jane** They arrested Tom.

**Sam** Again?

**Jane** Should we do anything?

**Sam** Nope.

**Jane** He sat in the doorway of Sainsbury's and yelled for an hour.

**Sam** Didn't the police stop him?

**Jane** Well, they arrived soon enough, but they couldn't move him.

**Sam** Why not.

**Jane** He was covered in red paint. Gloss.

*So are her hands.*

**Jane** Finally the police tried to lift him on to a blanket, but every time they began to lift, he started screaming that he had very brittle bones, a delicate skull, and a black belt in Tai Kwon Do. He's completely shameless.

**Sam** He's completely stupid. Everyone who comes here's bonkers.

**Jane** I've something to show you.

*She goes upstairs.*

**David** Andrew? You stupid bastard. / Grateful? You phone in a story . . . my story . . . and you're not even bloody well there. / That's not the point. You should have waited for the P.A report, that's the point. / I agree. It's a very simple story. Prime Minister opens ring road. Not much scope for inaccuracy. Unless of course she doesn't actually fucking open the God damn fucking ring road. She's in hospital, you dickhead, detached her bloody retina. Jesus, Andrew, I mean . . . don't you even listen to the news? / Look, next time I want a favour, do me a favour and don't do it.

*Puts phone down.* **David** *dials again.*

**Sam** Would you like to be in my film?

**David** I don't think so.

**Sam** You could have your eye poked out with a rivet gun.

**David** I'll pass, thanks.

**Sam** Or a stabbing? I've got a proper knife.

**David** Bob? / What can I say, Bob? / Yes, I got the story phoned in and it was the wrong bloody story and I'm very sorry . . . / Look, Bob, ask yourself why. Why would I fuck you up over this? / I know you did, but . . . Look, I was not pissed. / Well, you can talk. / That's as maybe, but this is a good story. / What? / Well no, not yet. / Bob, you don't hire and fire, so don't make idle threats; Peter's the one who hires and fires, Bob? . . . / Hi Peter. / Yes. / No, of course not. / What? / Oh come on, Peter, you don't mean that. Don't let Bob wind you up. Peter . . . Peter? Oh shit.

*He puts the phone down.*

**Sam** You shouldn't swear in front of me. I'm very impressionable.

**David** *opens a bottle of Scotch and swigs.*

**Sam** Have you seen 'The Evil Dead?'

**David** I used to work for them.

**Sam** *leaps up and puts a video tape on.* **Jane** *returns with the photo of* **David** *and questions* **Sam** *as he prepares the video.*

**Jane** Have you ever seen this man? Sam? Answer me.

**Sam** You mean David?

**Jane** You know him? He was here?

**Sam** Of course he was.

**Jane** Oh thank God, and thank you, Sam.

**Sam** Can you scream?

**Jane** What happened to him?

**Sam** You could be my leading lady if you can scream. Watch.

**Sam** *runs the video. They watch a decapitation.*

**David** That's disgusting.

**Jane** Lovely. Sam, answer me.

**David** How do they do that?

**Sam** He was here. Then he left.

**David** Invisible edit?

**Jane** Did he say where he was going? Please, Sam. I need to know.

**Brenda** *comes in with shopping.*

*Video off.*

**Brenda** Here we are then.

**Sam** Oh shit.

*He tries to tidy up.*

**Brenda** Oh, Sam. Look at the mess. And this horrible thing. I wish you'd grow up and out of all this. They said you would. When will you?

**Sam** It's just a hobby, that's all.

**Brenda** Do it in the shed then, where no one can see you.

**Sam** *goes out through the kitchen.*

**Brenda** I don't go in Sam's shed. It's horrible in Sam's shed. Thought I'd put a stop to this.

**Jane** It's hard to know where they get it from, isn't it? All this sex and violence.

**Brenda** Not from no one. Not from anywhere, not Sam.

**Jane** The TV probably.

**Brenda** No. He makes it up. It's all in his head. But that's alright. That's perfectly normal. Behaviour, that's all it is.

**Jane** Tea in the pot.

**Brenda** Lovely.

**Brenda** *leaves to get some.*

**Jane** *sits on the sofa,* **David** *rising just before she settles.*

**David** *goes upstairs. As he gets to the top* **Sam** *suddenly appears in front of him, screaming. He repeatedly plunges a knife into* **David***'s chest.*

**David** Jesus Christ. Fuck off.

**Sam** Were you frightened?

**David** I'll break your bloody neck for you.

*Enter* **Brenda** *with shopping.*

**Brenda** Here we are then. What's going on?

**David** Your son's a bloody lunatic.

**Sam** *stabs himself repeatedly, dies.*

**Brenda** Did you give him Smarties?

**David** If I was his father I'd give him a bloody good hiding.

**Brenda** They go funny on Smarties.

**David** Where is his father anyway?

**Brenda** Nowhere.

**Sam** Dead.

**Brenda** Not dead. Gone away, that's all.

**Sam** He's dead, or he'd come and see me. I reckon he's dead anyway. Don't sit down!

**David** *sits on* **Sam**'s *mask.*

**David** Oh sod it.

**Sam** You cracked it, you f . . . idiot!

**Sam** *leaves.*

**Brenda** Don't mind Sam. He's a good boy.

**David** Is Tom back yet?

**Brenda** Usually in the pub at lunchtime.

**Brenda** *goes into the kitchen.* **David** *drinks, then goes the same way as* **Sam**. *Pauses at the door, opens it very cautiously. As he relaxes and disappears,* **Jane** *jumps up from the sofa with a scream.*

**Brenda** (*off*) What's that?

**Jane** Something furry.

**Brenda** Happy hamster. Sam's always leaving him out.

**Brenda** *enters with tray.*

**Brenda** Did you catch him?

**Jane** I didn't try.

**Brenda** Oh well, he'll pop out again.

**Jane** *fingers the Encylopaedias.*

**Jane** Whose are these?

**Brenda** Oh. *Encyclopaedia Britannica.*

**Jane** Are they yours?

**Brenda** Fell off the back of a lorry.

**Jane** Do you use them at all?

**Brenda** No, never. I'd love to be bright but I'm thick. That thick I've no idea. There's one thing I do know mind you, that hardly no one else does. I know what a cephalic index is. I opened one of them. Just after they'd come one night I settled down and took one on my lap and opened it and I learned cephalic index. I don't remember nowt else, because I thought to remember cephalic index I'd better close the book to remember, then the phone, I forget . . . except the smell. Do you know what a cephalic index is?

**Jane** No.

**Brenda** No. No one does. No one ever has. But you know what's surprising? What's surprising is the number of times you can bring it up in conversation when you do know what it means. They smell lovely if you open them. But where to start? There's yards of it. But that's nice. It's nice to have it all in one. Knowledge. It's nice to know that there it all is. If there were the time.

**Jane** (*reading*) How wide your skull is, as compared to how long.

**Brenda** (*smiles*) Cephalic index. I talk to you. That's a turn up.

**Jane** Brenda, Sam said he recognised David.

**Brenda** No.

**Jane** He was very sure. He even said he liked him. That means you've been lying to me.

**Brenda** No.

**Jane** Brenda, I'm not cross, but I want to know why you're lying. Did something happen to him?

**Brenda** What do you mean?

**Jane** An illness, an accident, God knows.

**Brenda** No.

**Jane** I hope not.

**Brenda** No accidents around here. No pain, no nothing. No violence.

**Tom** *enters behind them, covered in red paint.*

**Tom** Hello.

**Jane** Jesus.

**Brenda** Oh, Tom!

**Tom** It's alright, Brenda, it's paint. It's only paint.

**Brenda** Oh look at you, Tom. Look at you. Look at him. He's out of his box, isn't he, Jane? You're out of your box you are.

**Tom** I am. And they're not going to get me back in.

**Brenda** Something wrong with his cephalic index.

**Jane** Just what I was going to say.

**Brenda** You ought to be locked up.

**Tom** I was.

**Jane** What are you out on, bail?

**Tom** No, I'm out because I can only use a Thompson-Kearney Facility Lavatory, so I demanded a Thompson-Kearney Facility Lavatory and they didn't have one, so they let me out.

**Jane** What *is* a Thompson-Kearney Facility Lavatory?

**Tom** Christ knows.

**Brenda** You need a bath.

**Tom** True.

**Brenda** I'll get the turps.

*She goes.*

**Jane** Did they hurt you?

**Tom** No. Surprisingly sensitive, the Cumbrian police. Did they bother you?

**Jane** No, I ran. I went to the pub. The pub round the corner.

**Tom** Oh?

**Jane** The manager recognised David's photo. Said he'd been in a couple of times. With you.

**Brenda** *returns with the turps. She begins to clean* **Tom** *down, starting with his hands.*

**Jane** Well?

**Tom** Well what?

**Jane** Why all this secrecy?

**Tom** I don't like talking to strangers. I got drunk once with a very attractive woman. Next day some friends of mine tried to put to sea and their dinghy sank. She was Special Branch.

**Jane** Well I'm not bloody Special Branch. And they don't waste their time investigating idiots who pour paint over themselves.

**Tom** They do if it's red paint.

**Jane** You're a political fanatic.

**Tom** And you're a political invention. Articulate, attractive female, non-rad Lib-fem, urban model, circa 1990.

**Jane** All I want is my husband!

**Tom** And eleven other endearing phrases. Just pull cord and release.

**Jane** What were you two involved in? A writer and a radical, a few miles from Sellafield. Have you been told to keep quiet? Did he find out something he wasn't meant to know?

**Tom** Look out!

**Jane** What?

**Tom** Flying pig.

**Brenda** Where?

**Jane** Answer me.

**Tom** There's nothing to know about Sellafield. No secrets; it's just an old irradiated nuclear plant with big cracks in it. It's killed every fish from here to Wales and it may well kill us all. It's a serious issue, not a red herring in this domestic murder mystery of yours.

**Jane** Who said anything about murder?

**Tom** You did.

**Jane** No I didn't.

**Tom** Shh!

**Jane** What?

**Tom** Speak quietly.

**Jane** Why?

**Tom** Brenda might be wired for sound.

**Brenda** Tom, keep still.

**Tom** Testing, testing . . .

**Brenda** Tom!

**Jane** You said murder.

**Tom** I was referring to the events taking place in your head. You're deliberately avoiding the simplest explanation.

**Jane** Which is?

**Tom** He's left you.

**Jane** No.

**Tom** Took off one morning and didn't come back.

**Jane** He wouldn't do that.

**Tom** Maybe he doesn't want to be found.

*Pause.*

**Jane** Was he with another woman? Is that what this is all about? It is, isn't it? Brenda?

**Brenda** Mmm?

**Tom** Get me to the bathroom eh, Brenda?

**Brenda** Right.

**Jane** He *was* here. So tell me what happened.

**Tom** That's not up to me.

**Brenda** *wheels* **Tom***, stops.*

**Brenda** He did stay.

**Tom** Brenda.

**Brenda** It's alright, Tom. He was on his own. He stayed a couple of days, then he left. That's all. We don't know where, do we, Tom?

**Tom** No. But you're right, Jane. He did discover something nasty up here. It was wearing his shoes.

**Brenda** *wheels him out.*

**Jane** *considers following them, but instead grabs her coat and leaves.*

**David** *comes in. He has been drinking steadily.*

**David** Tom! Tom!

**Tom** *emerges, miraculously clean.*

**Tom** Greetings, snoop.

**David** What can I say, Tom? Thank you. I phoned in the story. They held the front page. And rewrote the leader. Half page picture, splash headline: 'Power Protest Prospers'. Two columns, eight-point bold: 'The security of our nation's nuclear installations was severely tested today when a mad dwarf on wheels waggled a loofah at visitors to the Sellafield Exhibition Centre. The protest continued for all of two and a half minutes, by which time police hero Constable Plod had found the brake on the wheelchair and bravely pushed the lone protester into a bush. A government spokesman said we will never give in to terrorism or any brand of toiletry.'

**Tom** The trouble with sarcasm, David, is that eventually it replaces everything else.

**David** I've got nothing else now, you pathetic bastard. Except pneumonia. I've travelled two hundred miles, ruined a very good pair of shoes, and lost my bloody job! All for that futile little stunt.

**Tom** If you refuse to report it, yes of course it's futile.

**David** Where were the others? Where were the students in skeleton leotards and gasmasks? Where were the old ladies with snapshots of their grandchildren? Where were the lesbians? Where was Tony Benn?

**Tom** Everybody round here works for BNF.

**David** Then why bother?

**Tom** Somebody has to.

**David** Somebody. Your body?

**Tom** I'll have you know that two and a half million spermatazoa underwent a mammoth trial of strength and endurance to produce me.

**David** Well, God knows how yours won.

**Tom** Must have had a head start.

**David** Must have had a speedboat. Or maybe the others let him win. Maybe they had a policy of positive discrimination.

**Tom** I know I'm only one small voice. That's why I need you to amplify it.

**David** Well, you've nobbled the wrong horse. I needed a fucking good story, not a duckling on a dog's head. I've lost my job!

**Tom** You're a big disappointment to me.

**David** Well God, Tom, I'm so sorry.

**Tom** You're not what I expected. I expected a crusader. Someone who believed in something.

**David** A salary, that's what I believed in.

**Tom** Don't be facetious. You don't believe in anything.

**David** Well frankly, no. No, I don't.

**Tom** Why not?

**David** Time of life.

**Tom** What happened in your life to make it so deadly?

**David** That's none of your fucking business.

**David** *kicks the globe. Catches it. Staggers out.*

*Lights fade.*


Scene Five

*Lights up on the beach.*

**Jane** *sits watching the ocean.* **Buddy** *enters behind her.*

**Buddy** Hi.

**Jane** Ha!

**Buddy** I'm sorry.

**Jane** Christ. Sorry.

**Buddy** I made you jump.

**Jane** No, I'm just a bit jumpy.

**Buddy** I'm Buddy.

**Jane** I'm Jane.

**Buddy** Welcome to the beach, Jane.

**Jane** I saw you here this morning. And yesterday as I arrived. In fact every time I pass the beach, you're here.

**Buddy** And you're here too.

**Jane** I'm just passing through. You're always here. One person on the whole beach and when you get closer it's always you.

**Buddy** I like the beach. The tide here is very dramatic. It goes out a long way. You're not from around here, are you?

**Jane** Well, neither are you.

**Buddy** No, but I belong. Why are you here?

**Jane** I'm looking for a man. His name's David. He's disappeared.

*She hands* **Buddy** *the photograph.*

**Jane** Do you know him at all?

**Buddy** Shh.

**Jane** What?

**Buddy** Feel that?

**Jane** Feel what?

**Buddy** The tide's turning.

**Jane** You never saw him?

**Buddy** If you keep still enough you can feel the wave that turns the tide. We are 78 per cent water. We turn with it.

**Jane** The earth turns and the tide comes in. I can understand that. But it goes back out again.

**Buddy** Mmmhmm?

**Jane** Why doesn't it just keep on coming?

**Buddy** It's not the earth.

**Jane** What isn't?

**Buddy** It's the moon. If the earth was independent of the moon, then yes, the tide would drown us all.

**David** *enters, dribbling the plastic globe. His trousers are in a worse state. He carries a whisky bottle. He is very drunk.*

**Buddy** What sort of a man was your husband?

**Jane** Well, he was . . . Um . . .

**David** Fuck them all.

**Jane** He was a nice man.

**David** Shit heads. As Sinclair takes it down the wing.

**Jane** Articulate. Patient. Gentle.

**David** *boots the globe.*

**David** And it's there! Fuck them all. Sinclair! England! Sinclair! England!

**Jane** A very English man, really. Not as in typically English, as in . . . English, you know.

**Buddy** But what sort of man was he?

**Jane** He was . . . my husband. He was a nice man. He was a bit . . .

**Buddy** What?

**Jane** Well, like everyone else nowadays. You know.

**Buddy** Depressed or dangerous?

**Jane** No. No. He was a good man. Honest and upright.

**David** *falls over.*

**Buddy** Did he drink?

**Jane** No. Well, a bit. Not much.

**Buddy** He sounds almost perfect.

**Jane** Yes.

*Pause.*

**Jane** Well, nobody's that. He was a bit . . .

**Buddy** What?

**Jane** Nothing.

**Buddy** A bit what?

**Jane** Immersed.

**Buddy** Immersed?

**Jane** I loved him very much.

**Buddy** Immersed in what?

**Jane** Himself.

**Buddy** Ah.

**Jane** Like a lot of intelligent people.

**Jane** *looks out to sea.*

**David** *is now the one on the beach with* **Buddy**.

**David** The people are stupid. What's your name, friend?

**Buddy** Buddy.

**David** What's your name, buddy?

**Buddy** That's my name.

**David** American?

**Buddy** Once upon a time.

**David** What was I talking about?

**Buddy** The British.

**David** That's right. This is what I have learned in my thirty-odd years about the British people. I mean the mass of them. The Great British mass. Is fundamentally and irrevocably stupid. 70 million of them without an original thought in their heads. I have spent my life attempting to raise the consciousness of this mass. I have implored and encouraged. I have used words of few syllables. I have attempted to communicate about the state of the world in the hope that the mass might begin to change it. 3 million of the dozy sods read me. In 3 million ears and out the other 3 million. Another 3 million of them don't read anything at all.

And another 3 million, did you know this? Can't read! Don't be fooled by the people you rub shoulders with in wine bars and with whom you ardently discuss the dismantling of the Welfare State and what's coming down from Stratford. Don't be fooled into forgetting that most of the country is talking and thinking about Linda Lusardi's tits and another honest copper murdered by another gang of black rapists. Don't be fooled into believing the country is actually populated by people who can actually think!

**Jane** He was a thinker.

**David** Drink?

**Jane** I used to think he thank . . .

**Buddy** I think you're drunk.

**Jane** . . . thunk?

**David** I think so too.

**Jane** Too much for his own good.

**David** We drinkers, I mean thinkers, are in a minority of a majority so overwhelming in their mental simplicity, in their dull thick-headedness that our own tiny spark of intellectual capacity would be swamped and extinguished by them in an instant if it were not for the vile gas of privilege and dare I say it? superiority, that helps us keep rising to the top, like the creamy farts we are.

**Jane** He was a socialist. When I met him. Full of hate for his father; aimed it all at everything his father stood for, and my family too as a matter of fact. I'm a bit of a lost cause actually, marrying him. I'll be sorry, but I'm not.

**David** It's the premise that all men are equal that dangles our balls in the Tory vice. It's patently obvious that all men are not equal. I mean, you may well be a better . . . beach bum than I am. I am not equal to you in the accomplishments of beach bummery perhaps. And I can't drive a wheelchair like

Tom. And if our personal wheelcount or our collections of flotsam and jetsam were a measure of success and happiness in this world, then you might be both of you, top of the heap. However. But. Ultimately. A knowledge of these things is not worth two good arms and two good legs and money in the bank. Equality is a false premise. Teach them what you like; some brains remain bigger than others. And some women have archetypal playground bodies and others I personally wouldn't touch with a ten-foot pole. The point about life is, and this is the point; it isn't fair. It isn't even women and children first. It's every man for himself.

**Jane** He was a very happy man. When we met. But something died inside him, and all his words were rotting.

**Buddy** You believe in the inequality of man?

**David** I believe in life as it is lived.

**Buddy** But life is lived appallingly. Inequality is not a fundamental truth. It's a by-product of defining ourselves. Somewhere along the line, God forgive us, we decided to be tall, white, male and rich, and to hell with Them.

**David** Three out of four. Will I go to heaven?

**Jane** It was hope, it was his hope that died.

**Buddy** What do you do for a living?

**David** I am a small cog in a large machine that tells people what to think.

**Jane** He was a writer.

**David** The machine is a liar, of course.

**Jane** A good writer, too.

**David** And whichever way it turns, the smallest cog is as guilty as the mainspring. I think I'll drown myself.

**Buddy** Sit right where you are and you will.

*A wave laps* **Jane**'s *feet.*

**Jane** Arrgh!

**Buddy** You gotta watch the sneaky little ones there.

**Jane** Thanks for the warning.

**David** *gives the globe to* **Buddy.**

**David** Here.

**Buddy** Thank you. Don't you want it?

**David** I don't know what the fuck to do with it!

**David** *staggers off.*

**Jane** When I was a kid I'd try to pick a wave way out in the distance; the wave that would grow and grow and just keep growing I suppose, and drown us all. All my waves were disappointments. Have you been here long? In England?

**Buddy** A while.

**Jane** Where did you come from?

**Buddy** Montana, via the moon.

**Jane** Uh huh. And before you stood on the beach all day, what did you do?

**Buddy** I worked for NASA. I was an Apollo astronaut.

**Jane** A what?

**Buddy** An astronaut. Somebody had to be.

**Jane** What's your name?

**Buddy** I'm the one whose name no one can remember.

**Jane** *gives a laugh, stifles it. Looks at him. He is entranced, open. He is mad as a hatter, or telling the truth.*

**Jane** How was the moon?

**Buddy** Very fine. Still feel the pull.

**Jane** I have to go now. It's getting dark.

*She walks away.*

**Buddy** Here.

*Throws her the globe.*

**Jane** What for?

**Buddy** You'll think of something.

**Jane** *goes cautiously.*

**Buddy** It was not my help they wanted, nor each other's. I guessed they were going through a separation not so much from each other as from the selves they had once loved. A journey of the soul is measured not with maps and compass points but with meetings, and encounters not with fellow travellers, but with those you pass. They are there to teach you a little of the landscape they know better. David's journey was to be the most treacherous, especially as he returned home that evening to Brenda's house. Because at Brenda's house that evening, he was to meet the Devil.

*Lights Fade.*

# Act Two

Scene One

*Night.* **Jane** *returns home from the beach. The house is empty, deathly quiet. The room is quite dark, but the stairwell is lit. A video camera on a tripod points towards the stairwell.*

*The* **Parrot** *gives a low rumbling squawk.*

**Jane** Just say it will you? Even if you don't mean it.

*She strokes the* **Parrot**. *It bites her finger.*

**Jane** Ow!

*A bump from upstairs.*

**Jane** *investigates, cautiously.*

**Jane** Sam?

*The head comes bouncing down the stairs and lands at her feet. She picks it up.*

**Jane** Very funny, Sam. But once is enough.

*Getting no reply, she turns away from the foot of the stairs.*

**Sam** *springs up from behind the sofa.* **Jane** *screams.*

**Jane** You sod.

**Sam** Fishing line, see? Simple.

**Sam** *detaches the video camera from its tripod.*

**Jane** Am I on that?

**Sam** Do you mind?

**Jane** Yes.

**Sam** I have to work at night. Avoid my mother.

**Jane** Sam, how long was David here?

**Sam** Who?

**Jane** Don't start. David.

**Sam** Oh, him.

**Jane** Where did he go?

**Sam** Will you give me a hand?

**Jane** Sam. Did he tell you where he was going?

**Sam** Maybe. Help me first.

**Jane** Two minutes.

**Sam** Brilliant. This bloke's head gets chopped off at the top of the stairs, right? I can't shoot that bit yet. Then it rolls to the bottom, right?

*He hands her the head.*

**Sam** Hold that.

**Jane** Is this paint?

**Sam** No.

**Jane** Good.

**Sam** It's pig's blood.

**Jane** Oh God.

**Sam** Just stand halfway up the stairs and when I say 'action', roll it down.

**Jane** Why is there a worm instead of an eye?

**Sam** The worm popped his eye out.

**Jane** Ask a silly question.

**Sam** It's a worm lives inside me and when I whisper in your ear or kiss you or anything, you've had it because the worm crawls in. It's a very long worm and it pierces your eardrum and slides around inside your nasal passage and pops your eyes out from behind. You can grab it then if you're quick, and pull it out through your eye socket like a tapeworm. Or if you're in a lot of pain you just give up and decapitate yourself. Alright, standby.

**Jane** What about the mess?

**Sam** Action!

*She drops the head.* **Sam** *shoots, handheld.*

**Jane** Now tell me about David.

**Sam** Could you aim more for the banisters?

**Jane** Sam!

**Sam** *hands her back the head.*

**Sam** He was alright, David. He was quite useful for a while.

**Jane** How?

**Sam** Don't you recognise him?

*She drops the head.*

**Jane** Jesus.

**David** *enters with a hard white mask on. One eye hole.*

**David** (*distinct*) When the hell can I take this off?

**Sam** Soon. Careful.

**Sam** *leads* **David** *to the sofa and sits him down.*

**Sam** The harder it grows the more brittle it gets, so don't move your face.

**David** How the bloody hell could I move my face?

**Sam** He let me plaster of Paris him. Nobody else would.

**Jane** And then?

**Sam** He left.

**Jane** In one piece? Or did you dismember him first?

**Sam** Don't be ridiculous. It's only latex.

**David** Aaargh!

*He leaps up from the sofa and turns in a circle. Happy hamster has paid another visit to the outside world.*

**Sam** David!

**David** What the fuck was that?

**Sam** Keep still. What's the matter?

**David** A rat. There's a rat in the sofa.

**Sam** A what?

**David** A rat.

**Sam** Not a rat, it's a hamster that's all. Stop moving about. Sit down.

**David** Have you got it?

**Sam** God, hold on.

**Sam** *plunges his arm down the back of the sofa. Fails to find the hamster, but brings up a dusty video cassette, which he blows the fluff off and leaves on the arm of the sofa.*

**Sam** Alright, got it. You can sit down now.

**David** You got it.

**Sam** Want to feel?

**David** No.

**Sam** *rattles a cage, pretending to put the hamster in.*

**David** Right.

**David** *sits.*

**Jane** His nose is wonky.

**Sam** His nose was wonky.

**Jane** His face is too fat. Bloated. As if he'd drowned.

*Enter* **Tom**.

**Tom** Sam.

**Sam** Shit.

**Tom** Now what in hell do you think you're doing?

**Sam** She's asleep.

**Tom** That is no excuse.

**Sam** I'll clean up the mess.

**Tom** You made the mess, Sam, that's what I'm objecting to. (*To* **Jane**.) And what are you? A Welsh scrum half? Get it cleaned up, Sam. Before you give your mother a coronary.

**Sam** Oh, Tom.

**Tom** Do as you're told. It's a wild goose chase anyway, Sam. How are you going to edit this epic? Scissors and sellotape?

**Sam** You're not my father.

*Exit* **Sam**.

**David** Sam. This is very boring. Sam.

**David** *finds the video tape under his hand*.

**Jane** I'm sorry, I sort of encouraged him.

**Tom** Sam has certain morbid interests it would be best to discourage.

**Jane** Perfectly normal isn't it? Kids and sex and violence. One day it's postman's knock and the next it's murder in the dark.

**Tom** Go to bed.

**Jane** As soon as you've told me where he went.

**Tom** We don't know.

**Jane** How am I supposed to believe that when you lied about knowing him, you lied about his being here . . .

**Tom** *turns to go*.

**Jane** I'm not leaving.

**Tom** There are things it's not my place to tell you.

**Jane** Well, they're the things I need to know. Aren't they?

**Tom** *leaves.* **Jane** *throws the head at his closed door.*

**David** *has managed to get a video into the machine and has sat himself in front of the telly. Using the remote control, he switches on.*

**Jane** *goes upstairs.*

*On the TV, a few seconds of 'Life on Earth' about whales.*

*Bad video edit (hiss and colour-buzz); short burst of soap credits.*

*Bad video edit, short burst of BBC sex drama.*

*Bad video edit and into old home video. Cheap end of the market colours. A young **Sam** fools around for the camera.*

*Bad video edit into static shot. The camera pointed at a sofa. For a moment the sofa remains empty and then **Michael** enters the frame, and sits in big close up.*

**Michael** *is bearded, and has a slight stammer. A nervous twisting of the neck. Quiet torment beneath a sad exterior.*

**Michael** Um. I can't say I'm sorry. Not that I'm not. But . . . I think I understand something now. Part of it. Last night I, um . . . That's um . . . I were in her bedroom she had a single bed with a plastic top with brass pins and candlewick. I'd done it to her. I were still doing it. She were gone, but I were making it worse.

**David** *peels his mask off.*

What's the point in being sorry? I'd been needing to make it worse and worse, which I never could understand. Something . . . There was a wardrobe door swung open and shoes fell out. Earlier. In the door was a mirror. I reached round for my Phillips' I think and I saw my foot in the mirror. My foot and hers in the mirror, for real. I could see it for real, my foot and hers. I dragged her down the bed 'til I could see her in the mirror. And me, in the mirror, and I finished, watching in the mirror . . .

**Brenda** *appears and stares in horror at the television. Shocked to the bone.*

**Brenda** No!

*She rushes to the sofa, finds the remote control. Freeze frames the picture.*

**David** You're Brenda. Jesus.

**Brenda** *is mesmerised by the silent picture long enough for* **David** *to take the remote from her. He starts the tape again and Brenda collapses, her hands to her ears.*

**Michael** And when I were finished I was finished. Satisfied, like I'd never been. Inside. Watching in the mirror, see, it's somehow made it real. And I felt good. And tonight, I'd just started on another and it was so real I didn't have to. And I stopped. I think it might be over now. I'm sorry.

*Static.*

**David** *turns to look at* **Brenda**.

**Brenda** When they'd taken him they took me upstairs and showed me his box. Said when did I know. Said I never knew. Opened his box. Made me look in. Said recognise that? Said no. Screwdriver. I didn't recognise nothing. I didn't know nothing. Said pull the other one, one of them. But no, I never knew.

**David** You're Brenda.

**Brenda** And Sophie doesn't know. And Sam was far too young. It's not even in the past for them. It never was, and mustn't be.

**David** That was Michael Armstrong, wasn't it? And you're Brenda.

**Brenda** And no one round here, neither.

**David** You're a legend, do you know that? Not one statement, not one photograph, no one on the Street managed to track you down, not before the trial, not during the trial, and not after the trial. You're a legend.

**Brenda** I'm just me, please.

**David** It was that bloody priest. Nobody could get further than that bloody priest.

**Brenda** He was kind. I never even went to church. But he did it all for me. Sold the house in Gosforth. This place was cheaper. Had some left over. Run out now.

**David** Can I have this?

**Brenda** No!

**David** Do you realise what it's worth?

**Brenda** No. Where did it come from?

**David** Do you realise how much money you could make?

**Brenda** No, please. Leave us alone.

*She takes the tape.*

**David** Brenda, trust me. I'm not some tabloid hack, I'm a serious . . . Brenda!

*She runs upstairs.*

**David** *thinks for a moment, then picks up the phone and dials.*

**David** Bob? It's David. / Yes I know it is but I thought you might like to know how the story turned out. / You're going to care, you are, because it's immense. / It's completely exclusive and it's gold dust. Unfortunately for you I'm not on salary so it's going to cost the paper an arm and a leg. / Because Bob, if you won't others will, believe me. With a story like this I can go to anyone I like. / Fine. If that's the way you feel. But Bob . . . don't you think you should have a quick word with Peter before I do? Just in case? / (*Smiles.*) I think you're being very sensible, Bob. I'll call you tomorrow. Or on the other hand, I might not.

*Puts phone down.*

**David** Thank you, God.

*Lights fade.*

Scene Two

*Someone moves around the darkened room.*

**Tom**'s *door opens and a shaft of light reveals* **Brenda**.

**Tom** (off) Brenda?

**Brenda** Tom.

**Tom** It's three o'clock in the morning. What are you doing?

**Brenda** I'm checking the animals, Tom.

**Tom** The animals are fine.

**Brenda** Are they alright, Tom?

**Tom** They all survived.

**Brenda** Because I dream of carnage now.

**Tom** Nasty word, Brenda.

**Brenda** Nasty dreams, Tom. Those gerbils, drowning in that mucky green aquarium. Neon tetras flopping on the floor of the mouse's cage. Budgie flapping up against the wires because its cage has got the cat in it.

**Tom** It's alright now, Brenda. You're safe, the kids are safe, the animals are safe.

**Brenda** In these dreams it always bursts and that aquarium holds a houseful of water. Drowns us skin and bones and fur and feathers. Lumps of catfood floating past the TV, floating. Cop shoots the darkie bobbing up and down past lovely old dog, gives up his doggy paddle didn't you? Goes under then.

**Tom** You'll not see him again.

**Brenda** My Mickey?

**Tom** Or David.

**Brenda** I never drown. Sometimes on the arm of the armchair, clinging on, claws out, waterlogged. Living room's an old canal by now. I'm a soaked and skinny old cat clinging on.

**Tom** *notices that she has a video tape in her hand.*

**Tom** Brenda?

**Brenda** And the aquarium floats by. The lights and the pump are still on; drying it out.

**Tom** Is that the tape?

**Brenda** Dry as a bone inside, it floats by. Fish lie on the rocks, drying out, curling up, last glimpse of all the water outside the glass. Little fossil house floating by with the furniture and the mothercare stuff and my comfortable shoes.

*He takes the tape from her.*

**Tom** Why don't we throw it away?

**Brenda** No.

**Tom** You don't want it.

**Brenda** Hide it, Tom.

**Tom** Alright.

**Brenda** Hide it well away, Tom, please.

**Tom** You should get to bed.

**Brenda** No. Staying down.

**Tom** Shall I make you some tea?

**Brenda** That'd be nice.

**Jane** *comes downstairs in her dressing gown.*

**Jane** I heard voices.

**Brenda** That was us. Me and Tom.

**Jane** Have you got an elastoplast? I can't stop bleeding.

**Tom** I'll get you one.

**Tom** *goes into the kitchen.*

**Jane** I think I owe you an apology. I'm not usually this paranoid. You say he just left; I've no reason not to believe you. I suppose I should just go home. I suppose.

**Brenda** I know. Home can be lonely. This sofa.

**Jane** Yes?

**Brenda** There's tears here, see. You can hardly see, but look. Cried them tears, so I know. Little tear stain. Look.

**Jane** *leans over to look closely.* **Brenda** *takes her bloodied finger and presses it on to the fabric.*

**Brenda** And blood. And . . . shh . . . look. Come. That's come, under there. Mickey's come, see?

**Jane** Who's Mickey?

**Tom** *returns.*

**Brenda** Got most of the paint off, didn't we, Tom?

**Jane** So I see.

**Tom** Except the important bits. They're still red.

**Jane** You mean your politics.

**Tom** I mean my bollocks. I've scoured everything else but my bollocks are sacred.

**Jane** *laughs, embarrassed.*

**Tom** Why don't you look at me?

**Jane** I am. I do. Don't I?

**Tom** Not as hard as you want to.

**Brenda** Go on, look at him.

**Jane** Alright, I'm looking.

**Tom** Look harder.

**Jane** I am looking. Really. Look, I'm looking.

**Tom** Harder.

*She looks very hard. Turns away embarrassed. Looks again. He raises his arm. She looks at it very closely. He smiles. She smiles.*

**Brenda** See?

**Jane** What's it like?

**Tom** What?

**Jane** Your life.

**Tom** It's like being trapped in a stop-action cartoon, like a plasticine man waiting for the animator to move you just enough for the next frame. If you move yourself, you fuck up the sequence, which pisses off the animator who pummels you into a lump again. Back behind the bars of who you are.

**Jane** But that's how I feel. That's how I've felt all my life.

**Tom** Here we are then. Both in the same canoe.

**Jane** Without a paddle.

**Tom** Or a canoe. Well, thank you. I was feeling a bit low but that's really cheered me up.

**Jane** I'm sorry.

**Brenda** Tom doesn't dwell.

**Tom** Ah, but I do. I shouldn't, but all creatures that on Earth do. Dwell.

**Jane** You're right, you shouldn't.

**Tom** You're right, I'm right. I really shouldn't. Let's go somewhere exciting with disabled access! Let's go to the library! Get them to break out the ramp. Let's go take a discreet piss behind the big wide door.

**Jane** I thought you campaigned for big wide doors and ramps.

**Tom** Yes. Into pubs, not fucking theatres. Into brothels and dogtracks, not the bloody town hall. (**Jane** *laughs*.) I make too many jokes. It's a dead giveaway. If jokes could kill I'd be a mass murderer.

**Jane** And are you?

**Tom** I thought we'd decided he was assassinated by the Central Electricity Generating Board.

**Jane** I know! I'm sorry.

**Tom** Do we look like murderers?

**Jane** It's not you I'm scared of, it's finding him. Being in a room I know he's been in that I've never been in with him, it's as if I made him up. All I've got is this memory of someone I loved but haven't yet met. If I don't find him soon he'll be a stranger. Did you get to know him?

**Tom** Eventually.

**Jane** How was he?

**Tom** Alive.

**Jane** He'd not been coming home. Not making love. Not loving me. That's all. Didn't love me. Anyone. And it made him furious, inside.

**Brenda** That look on his face.

**Jane** Did he tell you? Did he tell you what happened?

**Tom** Yes he did.

**Jane** What was it?

**Tom** You were there.

**Jane** But inside him? What happened?

**Brenda** Best not to know. I never.

**Brenda** *rises and swiftly climbs the stairs.* **David** *comes down them, she turns and tries to escape him, back into the living room.*

**David** Brenda? How would you like to earn ten thousand pounds?

**Brenda** What for?

**David** Some stories. Some memories. And the tape.

**Brenda** You mean in the papers?

**David** Yes.

**Brenda** (*very alarmed*) No!

**David** A serious article, maybe a short series.

**Brenda** No! No. I don't, I w . . . w . . . wouldn't w . . .
w . . .

**David** Brenda, don't get excited. I'm just making you
an offer.

**Brenda** No.

**David** Listen.

**Brenda** No!

**David** Listen!

**Brenda** I love my girl. I do. She's sunshine to me, my girl.

**David** Brenda, I understand . . .

**Brenda** You don't understand. Sophie and Sam don't know.
Sophie and Sam mustn't know, because I know, and I know
life's not worth living, it's not, if it wasn't for Sophie and Sam
and not knowing.

**David** Others need to know.

**Brenda** I never knew.

**Tom** What happened between you two?

**Brenda** All I ever knew was . . .

**Jane** Nothing.

**Brenda** Him, that's all.

**Tom** Tell me.

**David** But how can we ever know? Our loved ones.

**Jane** Never.

**David** Or ourselves?

**Tom** Ever?

**Jane** No.

**Jane** *cuts herself off from* **Tom**.

**David** That's what I want to explore.

**Brenda** Tom!

**David** Shh. Brenda . . .

**Tom** *enters* **David**'s *time scheme*.

**Tom** What? What's the matter?

**Brenda** He wants to tell, Tom. He wants to tell about my Mickey.

**David** Your words . . .

**Brenda** Tell him not to, Tom.

**David** The truth.

**Tom** Absolutely not, David.

**Brenda** I told you not to have him here.

**Tom** I'm sorry.

**David** Let's talk this through calmly. Let me tell you what I envisage.

**Tom** No.

**David** Before you dismiss it out of hand.

**Tom** Think what you're doing.

**David** Brenda will be fine.

**Tom** Brenda will not be fine.

**David** She'll make a lot of money.

**Tom** Christ, David. I can't for the life of me understand why Brenda's peace of mind is worth less to you than a few columns of filthy newsprint.

**David** Look, I'm a journalist. It's what I am.

**Tom** It's not all you are.

**David** I will not let compassion stand in my way here.

**Tom** You don't even like your job.

**David** I have to tell this story.

**Tom** Why?

**David** Because it's mine. I want to write about him. Whatever it was inside him.

**Brenda** Why?

**David** Because it happened.

**Brenda** Tom. That look on his face.

**Tom** Happened to whom?

**David** I could write a book. Forget the papers, I could write a book.

**Tom** Why this morbid fascination?

**David** Because it's part of us.

**Tom** What is?

**David** Whatever it was spilt from Brenda's husband! That sticky black darkness! It's in us all for Christ's sake, isn't it?

**Tom** All of us?

**David** Isn't it?

**Tom** In you, you mean?

*Pause.*

**David** Yes.

**Tom** Then maybe it's yourself you should be writing about.

*Pause.*

**Tom** Tell your own story.

**David** I don't have one.

**Tom** I don't believe you. If you want Brenda's story you might at least have the guts to tell your own.

*Pause.*

**David** It's a very short story.

**Tom** Tell us.

**David** She was . . .

**Tom** Yes?

**Jane** I was lying in the bath. This was the night before he left. We'd been arguing. About something. The bathroom floor I think. He left it wet. I dry it.

**David** I no longer love my wife, that's all.

**Jane** I was in the bath with my eyes closed. I heard him come in, I heard his electric shaver, then silence. I thought he must be looking at me. I hoped he was.

**David** It was as if she'd tied barbed wire round my heart. Nothing I did was right. Nothing I did was enough. Then there was a moment . . .

**Jane** His hand gripped my ankle, then he tugged and I went under. Opened my eyes, my mouth, and coughed what air I had up into my face and gone. I had no air until I'd struggled up on to my elbows, gasping, coughing . . . fire and water down my nose. Then he let go.

**David** I discovered that cold, black nugget in me. I stood over the bath. The cuff of my shirt was sopping wet.

**Jane** I prayed for him to smile. A smile to dilute the fear I felt. But for a second; who knows how long; no smile. Just surprise on his face and hate behind his eyes, hate that scampered back into his head to hide.

**David** The good boy that I am. The sensitive man. My intellect. My humour. My life. A sort of joke.

**Jane** Then he smiled. It was a joke.

**David** She thought it was a joke, the drowning.

**Both** But it wasn't.

**Jane** He'd meant it.

**David** We laughed it off.

**Jane** He left the room. I dried myself.

**David** Since then I've found it hard to care. About her, me, anyone. I have to know who Michael was, And why.

*He goes upstairs*

**Jane** I care what happened to him. I can't help but care. But I don't know why. I'm going for a walk.

**Jane** *leaves.*

*The sound of typing from upstairs.*

**Brenda** *hears it. It grows louder, more insistent, until it's an exaggerated death rattle of noise.*

**Brenda** Tom?

**Tom** It's alright, Brenda.

**Brenda** Make him stop, Tom. Make it not, Tom, shall I? It was all over. How can I make it all over again?

*Lights fade.*

Scene Three

*Moonlight up on the beach.* **Jane** *curled up, using the half inflated globe as a pillow.*

**Buddy** *arrives.*

**Buddy** Aren't you going to sleep in your bed?

**Jane** I'm sleeping here.

**Buddy** You'd better not.

**Jane** I'm sleeping right here.

**Buddy** Not if I were you.

**Jane** Well, you're not and I shall.

**Buddy** On the beach? At high tide?

**Jane** A really deep sleep. See that wave?

**Buddy** Down below the night tide?

**Jane** That wave there?

**Buddy** You wouldn't survive.

**Jane** That wave's mine.

**Buddy** Which one?

**Jane** The big one. It'll take us all.

*Pause.*

**Jane** Huh.

**Buddy** You'll have to wait a long time for the wave that doesn't break.

**Jane** If he's dead I wish I was. If he's somewhere nicer than dead, I still wish I was. And I wish he was.

**David** *appears on the beach, dressed to leave town. Thrusts a few typed pages at* **Buddy**.

**David** Buddy. Read this.

**Buddy** What is it?

**David** It's what I do.

**Buddy** *reads.* **David** *sits on his suitcase.*

*In the living room,* **Sam** *is asleep.* **Brenda** *brings the sleeping* **Sophie** *and lays her down to join him. Then she begins to stack the animal cages around the gas fire.*

**David** That's just the introduction. Can you imagine? That's the house. You'd never know. It's just a rough draft. What do you think?

**Buddy** What do you care?

**David** An opinion. It's an important story, don't you think?

**Buddy** How does it end?

**David** It doesn't end. Whatever pain gets passed around, life goes on, doesn't it?

**Brenda** *turns on the gas fire without lighting it. Settles down to die.*

**Buddy** How does she feel about it?

**David** Who?

**Buddy** This Brenda, who else?

**David** She's . . . concerned, naturally. She'll be OK. So what do you think?

**Buddy** I think it's very powerful.

**David** Absolutely. That's what I wanted to hear.

**Buddy** Tell me, are the English all so brim full of this obsessive despair?

**David** I've got a train to catch.

**Buddy** *nods*.

**Buddy** Do you like to swim?

**David** God no, I hate it. In fact I can't. As for the sea, it terrifies me. I never go near it.

**Buddy** Never?

**David** No.

**Buddy** Then how come you're so close to drowning?

**David** I'm not, am I?

**Buddy** *grabs him, trips him, holds his head under the water.*

**Buddy** Sure you are. You're way out of your depth, boy. Can you taste the salt? Can you feel the cold?

*Lets* **David** *up*.

**David** Jesus. You're out of your mind.

**Buddy** These are just the shallows.

**David** I could have drowned. I can't get on a train like this. I'll have to go back and change.

**Buddy** Good idea.

**David** *grabs his manuscript and suitcase and goes.*

**Buddy** (*shouts*) Ocean's all around you, boy, whether you like it or not. Only compassion will keep you afloat!

**Jane** You can murder me if you like, but don't fold me up and hide me in some awful cupboard.

**Buddy** You sound a little depressed.

**Jane** When I was a kid I used to eat cheese at bedtime for the nightmares. Maybe that's why I came. Maybe I need a murder mystery in my life.

**Buddy** There's no excuse for being depressed. You want not to be depressed?

**Jane** Yes, I want not to be depressed.

**Buddy** Then get back inside your body. Get your body back on earth and your head back on top of it.

**Jane** I don't understand you.

**Buddy** Depression is a schism between the body and the mind; the blood and the electric. You have to get back inside yourself. Go jump in the ocean. You will feel wet when you come out, you might feel damn cold, but you sure as hell won't feel depressed.

**Jane** I wouldn't be depressed if he still loved me.

**Buddy** (*deadly serious*) Don't delude yourself, girl. In matters of sadness and the ocean tides, and voyagers, I know a little more than you.

**Jane** Then help me.

**Buddy** Have a swim.

**Jane** Help me!

**Buddy** Hit the water. Tell the ocean hello.

*She considers it, changes her mind.*

**Jane** Don't be ridiculous.

**Buddy** Do it!

*She instantly walks into the ocean, towards the audience. Up to above her knees.*

**Jane** Oh Jesus.

**Buddy** Go on.

**Jane** I can't!

**Buddy** You've got a deep sadness.

**Jane** But my feet!

**Buddy** You need deep water.

**Jane** It's freezing.

**Buddy** It's October.

**Jane** Come with me.

**Buddy** What do you think I'm crazy?

**Jane** I knew it! You're a paddler.

**Buddy** Jane.

**Jane** I knew you were just a paddler!

**Buddy** You know you have to do this.

**Jane** All mouth and rolled up trousers.

**Buddy** Now or never and it's NOW!

**Jane** Oh G-o-d!

**Jane** *runs into the water, immersing herself.*

**Jane** Oh God it's cold it's cold it's cold it's so cold.

**Buddy** Do you feel alive?

**Jane** You'll have to define 'alive'.

**Buddy** That's not easy. Do you know how hard that is? We flew a machine to Mars, do you remember, looking for life beyond all this. A magic laboratory. But early on, designing this Columbus, we realised we didn't know what we were looking for. Is all life carbon-based? No idea. Could be unimaginable. Out hunting tigers, miss a field full of rabbits. They knew life on Mars would be dissimilar to life here, but *how* dissimilar?

**Jane** Jesus, there are fish in here.

**Buddy** How not to underestimate the dissimilarity? A man called Lovelock looked into it.

**Jane** Can I come out now?

**Buddy** No. He analysed all known life forms on earth. And he realised they all had one thing in common. They were all responsible for altering their environment.

**Jane** I wish I hadn't.

**Buddy** We eat, we excrete, we breathe in, we breathe out. A changing environment is evidence of life.

**Jane** Buddy, it's all a bit academic to me, considering I'm about to freeze to death.

**Buddy** Listen. Lovelock had this tremendous shock. He realised that this empirical evidence of life pertained not only to any living thing on earth, but also to the crew of an ocean-going liner, a farm, a theatre, a city. A road haulage firm, a family, a country, a continent. The *earth itself*.

**Jane** I'm coming out now.

**Buddy** Not yet! By complete accident, Lovelock had defined the world as a living organism.

**Jane** That's what I am.

**Buddy** It's as alive as you are.

**Jane** Buddy, I want to stay that way.

**Buddy** Beg Pardon?

**Jane** I want to stay that way. Can I come out now.

**Buddy** Of course you can.

*She wades out of the ocean.*

**Jane** Oh God. Now it's colder out. You know what I wish?

**Buddy** What?

**Jane** I wish I'd taken my clothes off.

**Buddy** Do you see what it all means?

**Jane** I am too wet to think. Too cold to care.

**Buddy** *grabs her.*

**Buddy** Never too cold to care, Jane. Never. If the earth is a living being then interdependance is no optional phenomenon. We *do* connect, and each of us have a personal responsibility to the whole. Now how do you feel?

**Jane** Well funnily enough, absolutely fantastic. I feel . . . crystal. I still don't believe I did this.

**Buddy** We can each be baptised into the new age or stay shipwrecked on the old one. Life sends out the strangest invitations.

**David** *appears in the house. He sniffs the air and registers what's going on.*

**David** Jesus.

**Buddy** Sometimes the choice is so simple, there is no choice.

**David** *runs to the window and throws it open. Turns off the gas.*

*He helps* **Brenda** *up. She's groggy, but quickly recovers.*

**David** *goes to pick up* **Sophie**, *but* **Brenda** *tries to stop him.*

**David** It's alright. I'm not going to hurt her. I'm not going to hurt her. I'm not going to hurt you. Here. Take her outside. Quickly.

**Brenda** *does as she's told.* **David** *picks up* **Sam**, *who wakes and squirms a little.* **David** *carries him out.*

**Brenda** *returns.*

**Brenda** My animals.

**David** Alright! I'll save the animals. Get outside!

**David** *carries all the cages etc. out of the front door.*

*On the beach* **Jane** *is shivering.*

**Jane** Buddy, do you think I could remain true to the spirit of Aquarius if I wasn't soaking wet?

**Buddy** Mmm hmm?

**Jane** Because I have to get out of these things.

*She undresses. A moment of freezing embarrassment, then* **Buddy** *wraps his enormous coat around her. They settle.*

*First glimmer of dawn.*

**David** *and the family have left the house with two dogs, a cat, cages and a goldfish bowl.*

**Jane** What was it like being an astronaut, Buddy? What was it like on the moon?

**Buddy** Well, we went in search of what? Another life, new life forms. And there we were scuffing about in the darkness of the dust beneath our feet and found nothing and then I looked up and there it was. Life unrecognisable. It was up above us all the time. Here was a dead moon, but up there, the earth. A new life form, more complex than we'd ever imagined. All we had to do was live it.

**David** *and the family appear on another part of the beach.*

*In the distance, a ghostly glow from Sellafield.*

**Sam** *keeps his distance, tired but stoic.*

**David** She'll freeze. Here.

*Takes off his jacket for **Sophie**.*

**Brenda** Don't tell.

**David** I'm not going to tell. I promise.

**Brenda** Do you promise?

**David** Yes.

*He screws up his manuscript, tosses it.*

**Buddy** The earth exists now not beneath my feet but in my memory, and in my memory it is a jewel, a fluid crystal, the heart of a translucent, peaceful, and eminently wise creature. It beats for us. All we have to do is beat with it.

**Brenda** Used to be moonlight.

**David** Mmmhmm?

**Brenda** There used to be moonlight here. Can't feel the moonlight now, just the light from the 'lectric plant. My husband used to work there. His dad got him a job before he died. Leukaemia. He was in the papers. Not his name, but statistics. Mickey came home; he was late because the alarm went off on him and he had to shower twice. And the electric bill had come and we never had enough for that and then his mum came round and said his dad had died. And he wouldn't cry and sat there tight and looked at me and said, 'What are you crying for, you ugly cow, he was my dad.' 'God, you're an ugly cow,' he said, and then he went out. That night was the first one. I know what he did was wrong. But there's so much wrong about. That's killed children round here, and Michael's dad, and all those Russians, and that's not right. And the people round here, something in them's died living with all that. Living with all that, something's died in all of us.

**David** Hardly cause and effect though, Brenda.

**Brenda** What's that?

**David** The things you do . . . cause other things to happen.

**Brenda** Oh, no. I know. Just coincidence. But there's so much bad about now, it can't all be can it? Public and private. Good and bad's bigger than all that.

**Buddy** Lot of talk about destroying the earth. Heap of bullshit. We couldn't destroy it if we tried. All we could destroy is *ourselves*. And blow some dust the while into that great blue eye. And that great blue eye would blink and we'd be gone.

**Brenda** How do you feel?

**David** Alright. I feel good.

**Brenda** Good.

**Buddy** How do you feel?

**Jane** I don't know what to do.

**Buddy** Do what you feel.

**David** You know what it is? It's the head gets somehow separated . . .

**Jane** . . . Somehow separated from the heart.

**David** Doesn't it?

**Jane** *kisses* **Buddy**.

**Jane** I don't want to do that again.

**Buddy** That's alright, neither do I.

*They smile.*

**Buddy** I'd like to give you this.

**Jane** What is it?

**Buddy** It's not much.

*He gives her a box, smaller than a matchbox. She opens it. Inside, bits of crumbling grey rock, almost dust.*

**Jane** It's really lovely. That's really lovely, Buddy, thank you. A box of dirt.

**Buddy** Mmmhmm.

**Jane** Oh no.

**Buddy** Mmmhmm.

**Jane** Oh come on, it's not.

**Buddy** If it's not, throw it away.

**Jane** Look, I can't take this. If it is, I can't take it. Is it?

**Buddy** If you don't believe it is, then it may as well not be.

*She closes the box very carefully.*

**Jane** It's just a bit of earth, isn't it.

**Buddy** Would that make it any less valuable?

*He rises.*

**Buddy** Come on, I'll see you home.

*They leave the beach.*

**David** *moves away from* **Brenda**.

**Brenda** Where are you going?

**David** Walk along the beach.

**Brenda** It's hard to tell in this light if the tide's coming in. You could get cut off if the tide's coming in.

**David** What if it's going out?

**Brenda** Oh, then you'd walk all the up and around.

*And so* **David** *leaves.*

**Brenda** But what if it's not? What if it's not?

*Lights fade.*


Scene Four

*Sunrise.*

*Lights up in living room.* **Tom** *drinks coffee with* **Jane**, *who sits with her bag.* **Tom** *is dressed as a woman.*

**Tom** Brenda was the last to see him, and so you see how hard it would have been, to admit that and drag her back into the nightmare of police and gossip and some other man from some other paper.

**Jane** Do you think he drowned?

**Tom** There's more chance he beat the tide and just kept on walking.

**Jane** He hates walking. Where would he walk to?

**Tom** I think he realised he had some serious work to do. On himself.

**Jane** But he left me.

**Tom** Yes.

**Jane** A fine change of life. Leave the wife. Very original. What a shitheel. I mean seriously, isn't he? Stupid bastard.

**Tom** Well, he's not all bad.

**Jane** I know that, but he'll need more than heroic tales of hamster rescue when I see him again. Oh Christ. I might never see him.

**Tom** That's true.

**Jane** I'm a grown woman, it's absurd. I ought to be able to cope without one bloody man. Especially him. Why is it so hard?

**Tom** I've never understood why people get so painfully bound up with one person and remain so horribly disconnected from everyone else.

**Jane** A taste of heaven and a taste of hell. Why are you dressed as a woman?

**Tom** God, is that the time? I've got to get to the pub. They've got a stag lunch on.

**Jane** What are you, the cabaret?

**Tom** No, some poor half-naked woman is the cabaret. I am the raising of the consciousness! Bye bye.

**Jane** Bye.

**Tom** *leaves.*

*Lights up on the beach.* **David** *walks on, no jacket, no socks. A weary traveller.*

**Jane** *takes the box out of her pocket, and stirs the dust with her finger.*

**David** *takes his shoe off and pours from it a fine long trickle of sand.*

**Brenda** *comes on to feed the animals.* **Jane** *changes into walking boots.*

**Brenda** Oh. You're off then.

**Jane** Yes. Along the beach. David went north, didn't he?

**Brenda** Yes.

**Jane** Then I'll go south.

**Brenda** Don't want to catch him up then?

**Jane** Don't want to waste my life chasing him. Oh, by the way.

**Jane** *takes the half-deflated globe from her pocket. Blows it up.*

*At the same time* **David** *takes deep breaths of ocean air.*

**Jane** *hands the globe to* **Brenda**.

**Jane** I found this. For the kids?

**Brenda** Oh, ta. I wondered what had happened to that.

**Jane** *leaves.* **Brenda** *sits with globe. She walks the fingers on her right hand southwards, then the fingers on her left go north. They meet and intertwine, satisfied. Lights fade.*

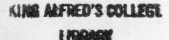
KING ALFRED'S COLLEGE
LIBRARY